The Rain Diaries

ROSIE GARNER was born, raised, and still lives in Nottingham. She has won prizes in many competitions and is widely published in magazines and anthologies. She has represented the East Midlands in two major arts projects; the 24:8 writers' tour and 3 Cities Create and Connect. She works in schools, libraries and for various other community based organisations. She has been a writer in residence in prison and for Nottingham City Transport.

The Rain Diaries

ROSIE GARNER

SALT

LONDON

PUBLISHED BY SALT PUBLISHING
Fourth Floor, 2 Tavistock Place, Bloomsbury, London WC1H 9RA United Kingdom

© Rosie Garner, 2010

The right of Rosie Garner to be identified as the
author of this work has been asserted by her in accordance
with Section 77 of the Copyright, Designs and Patents Act 1988.

Salt Publishing 2010

Printed and bound in the United Kingdom by Lightning Source UK Ltd

Typeset in Swift 9.5 / 13

ISBN 978 1 84471 518 3 paperback

1 3 5 7 9 8 6 4 2

To my mother
thank you for the strange and wonderful conversations.

Contents

Acknowledgements

My thanks to the editors of the following magazines and anthologies in which many of these poems have been published: *Dream Catcher, Envoi, Fin, Fire, Iron, Other Poetry, Poetry Nottingham, Staple, Stride Magazine, Smiths Knoll, The Coffee House, Tears on the Fence, Tremblestone, Not Just A Game — Sporting Poetry, The Nottingham Collection, Ware Competition Anthology, A Tale of 3 Cities, Words On Your Street Anthology*, Nottingham City Transport Website.

Other poems were specially commissioned for Lowdham Book Festival, and the 24:8 Writers' Tour of the East Midlands.

Thanks are over-due to poets and others for their friendship, advice and criticism over the years. Notable amongst these are, Sheelagh Gallagher (obviously), Cathy Grindrod for years of good advice, Barbara Lacey for commas and proof reading, Deirdre O'Byrne for anything from leafleting buses to buying the wine, Nigel Pickard for telling me which ones were printable and Steven Waling for the push.

Part One: Home Ground

Tigguocabauc

Asser wrote in his diary ". . . this day passed by Tigguocabauc . . ."

Late October in Nottingham.
Under the city, the caves
not god given wonders but our own.
We made them. We are Tigguocabauc,
the cave dwellers. We took antlers from hard ground,
held them fist firm, chiselled ceilings.
We took fire, pushed it into cracks,
made rock-fall, made space,
safe hiding for root grubbing winter.
We are the fire people, smoky eyed
see only flame on walls,
fire dancing, deer running.

Late October in Nottingham.
On the Forest, in the dark beyond the tram stop,
every Thursday is Fire Night.
Fire-eaters collect, cough columns of flame,
make gargoyles of those on the ground,
half watchers, half clansmen.
Fire on chains whizzes and whirls like buzz saws.
Flames in their hands dance like creatures
running from the hunt.
Mankind's first magicians swig paraffin tainted water
from plastic bottles.

Late October in Nottingham.
Deer bellow on Wollaton Park,
antlers clash and scythe the dying bracken.
Anger raises little clouds of steam,
treads in long-shot, long forgotten golf balls,
dies. After the rut,
antlers fall on frost-glazed ground.

We are the people of Nottingham,
cave makers,
fire-eaters.
Tigguocabauc.

Tigguocabauc—Latin/Welsh for house of caves or cave dwellers—Asser
was King Alfred's historian writing about Nottingham (Snottingham) in
868 AD.

[4]

Rain

Round here, the kids don't mind the rain,
don't try to put it off another day—
it's not as though they were expecting
impromptu river picnics
with hats.

They like the grit shooting up from puddles,
spray cans of mud for the sides of buses,
water spouts on down pipes
painting algae beards on walls.
The rain is one of them.

Flash flood in Basford;
bloke, halfway through his second pint,
sticks his head out the door of the Vernon Hotel,
sees the road gone, kids swimming at the crossings.
He goes back inside until his fifth
and finds the road's come back.
Just a high tide river dance across the tracks,
T-shirts draped on the automatic gates,
trousers looped around lamp posts.

Listen to the boy in class two,
muttering his incantation through the sweat of steam,
listen to them on the playgrounds,
hair streaming, half-blinded, half-drowned,
willing the sky to do its worst.

You'd think the kids round here
had *made* the rain.

Football on Vernon Park

A patient man,
he cups his hand against the wind,
lights his fag as the game gets underway.
Nods, *they'll shape up nice this year,*
the under eights.

With a lift of his arm and a call,
like a shepherd signalling his dogs,
he'll nudge a winger back in place,
picks out the sub,
sets him running down the field;
all the way,
if you want to play, you'll run.
He pinches off his fag and watches everything,
good lad, well done.

Across the pitch,
the knot of parents,
buggies, barking dogs.
Breath steaming for the first time this year,
trees leaning in to the end of summer.

And the boys standing
almost in their places,
hands on hips, rucked-up sleeves
that dangle back below their waists
as soon as they begin to run,
deadly serious, knowing the rules
and sticking to them.

You can see, in their cool appraisal of their game,
their shrugging acceptance of missed goals,
like shadows standing behind them,

the men they'll grow into.
He watches from the centre,
almost smiles, sees them now.

Chasing the Ace

Chasing the Ace in the bar of the Pear Tree,
flicking out cards, stopping the King,
this sad-eyed crew trying to laugh
on the other side of each other's faces.
As ever, Tracy won't stay still,
scrabbling around for her fags,
next week's club money
sloshing about in the bottom of her bag.

Chasing the Ace from three till eight
all of them wary of Johnnie and his mates
out in the car park—
little snot's taken off his tag again
god knows what he thinks he's up to.

All of them ignoring old Harry in the corner
flirting with the new couple,
feeding them a life story
stolen from war films.

And the night goes on,
Chase the Ace becomes 21s,
Julie goes to find Tracy
asleep on the bog
like a broken neck against the wall.
In the car park there's trouble brewing
some kid's lost his bike, he's
lying in the grass wiping blood from his chin.

But it's not enough and Johnnie's waiting for closing
when the saddos shuffle out.
He's ready for them tonight,
really ready,
looking for anything
that reminds him of home.

On Every Route

On every route, a line of poplars
like goose-quills slowing down the wind.
Methodists and Baptists advertise for souls,
God Washes Whiter!
Good or Evil? You decide!
Privet, crew cut
or long-legged, waving back.

Outside every Spa and Co-op,
teenagers and pensioners
eye each other warily,
minding the generation gap.

On every route —
the pawnshop
and cars on credit,
end of roll carpet
stacked on pavements.

On every route a long view opens up,
on cranes like masts on a choppy sea
or out the other way
to caterpillar lines of trees
bumping along the middle distance.

On every route
above every estate,
a kestrel thrums the air
and always
someone rooted to the ground
looking for it,
knowing that it's there.

We'll See After a Fortnight

MONDAY

The bus smells of mildew. People cough, sit too close.
He smooths clear plastic over his day ticket,
wishes he'd remembered his throat spray.

TUESDAY

This isn't for the bonus or the environment, it's his wife.
She thinks he needs the company of strangers, time
on his way to work to look out of the window.

WEDNESDAY

At what exactly? A petrol station boarded up
in memory of robberies and uninsured white vans,
the shantytown of allotments, the mucky Trent.

THURSDAY

He has a cold. Snow lands as rain. Some woman
holds the bus, waves him on with a silly grin.
Much too close. He pities the swans on the river.

FRIDAY

He's on the later bus; endures students from South Notts.
His wife's become convinced he'll join the quiz in Ruddington
which she calls Rud. She doesn't know what he's going through.

MONDAY

That woman again, but this time he holds the bus for her.
With dignity. He notices the green of County Hall, thinks
of all that copper, what it must have looked like new.

TUESDAY

His boys have it too easy with the school run. His wife
spoils them. He ignores an argument over his briefcase.
A lone sculler skates the Trent. He counts five ducks.

WEDNESDAY

Mobiles are intrusive, people ought to switch them off.
As they pass the fitness centre, he has a vision of himself
rowing on the spot, in Lycra. He suppresses it.

THURSDAY

He's given a green badge at work. Back home,
he fails to see what's funny, it's not as though he'll wear it.
Tomorrow, he thinks, he'll take his car.

FRIDAY

Flat battery. On the allotments, there's a goat, like a joke.
Behind it, a small tree bursting with blossom, white
as copy paper. And this is odd, it made him smile.

Speed Bumps

The driver of this bus
is young. He is feeling
every bump
for the man behind him
who tries not to cry out
and fails.

So the driver
slows,   right
down,
     grips the wheel
        as if he'd
            lift us
        over
   the
bumps   skirt
round them   but
traffic is bad,
    St. Albans Road
endless,   and this

is a white-knuckle ride
of a different kind.
The man's pain
unravels him. Each time
he cries, we
echo it.
We can't help it.

He will not stop apologising.
By the time he gets off
at the flats by the crossings
we wish
he'd never
got on.

Interglacial

On the corkscrew from Killisick, you
slide down roads like strips of thinnest skin
where house foundations only go so deep,
nubs of concrete set in mud and ancient coral reefs,
where once, between the ice sheets,
melt-water smashed its way against the grain
dragged grit and silt along new valley floors,
made Arnold into marshland, hot and humid.

Hippos grazed the night in water meadows
behind Sainsbury's, kept cool through underwater days
skimming over lily stems along the Daybrook.
Beneath the road today, you can hear
the chant of rock:
Red marl, Mercia Mudstone,
Sherwood sand, pebble beds.

Graveyard Shift

It did happen once, and not so far away,
Hell's Angels or some other desperate tribe,
drunk, stoned, and with the pub long closed,
climbed into the graveyard there,
and dug up the newly dead,

carried the pair of them up the road,
to arrange them as they might have been in life.
And they still live, those lads.
Not for anything would I have their dreams now.

Think of them, with the earth soft as potato beds
running off their clothes, boots ringing on tarmac
lit by a dog-bark moon. White faces wet with sweat
and laughter already half sick of themselves
carrying between them their prim burdens.

And think of those two souls, newly freed,
arrested in their headstrong flight
seeing themselves, too early in the morning,

sitting too close together, waiting for a bus
going the wrong way.

Part Two: Climate Change

Things I'd Like To Say

There are things I'd like to say but I can't find them anywhere
and thousands of miles away my daughter blows up a balloon
of words, bursts it, blows up another, bursts it.

She shelters in a suburb of Johannesburg whilst in town, police
are firing rubber bullets. She doesn't know what they are
protesting about. She cries over the killing of school children in
Soweto as though it only just happened.

My neighbour thinks our cat has gone senile because
he sleeps in the middle of the road, but the cat believes cars
will stop and wait for him to rise with his subtle stretching
walk. The driver shakes his head, the woman laughs.

The cat enjoys the company of my son and the scent of
cannabis. In the evenings, they lean together against the wall,
hidden by the fish shaped hedge. Small children point to the
hedge and say 'fish'.

There are too many pieces of paper. On the mantelpiece,
a pile of staples cling together like baby spiders.
There is a silver cup, with my son's name on it.
A sticky label inside it says 'do not remove from college.'

There will be something to say in the shed.
Leaves flatten against the window and rain raps on the roof,
petals plummet to the ground. Truth is too much of a luxury.
Hardly anyone can afford it.

My mother hauls down the drying-rack to fold clothes she hung
in her secret way. She is the only person who knows how to
hang them up. She has broken down her life
into hundreds of small tasks: many of them are invisible.

She has a way of tying rubbish bags, she shows me how, but it remains her secret. She explains things in a way it becomes impossible to remember unless you are nearly asleep or drunk.

In Kolkata, there is a market where men buy children. They come from the other side of the planet to this place and nobody believes it exists. In Delhi, a doctor buys kidneys so that men can show their scars to tourists.

My neighbour scowls up at the silver birch and fills bin liners with seeds. She thinks we ought to cut it down.
My husband was embarrassed. We didn't love each other carefully enough. There are things I'd like to say.

Black Box

But he hadn't listened to the pilot,
doesn't know how high they are flying,
how long it will take them to fall, only

the G force mouthing into his face, his
stomach shape shifting into his back
the startled eyes of the woman sitting next

to him with the angle of her head all wrong.
Odd how clearly he's thinking. Odd
that he finds it odd.

In the hold is the box his father gave him,
holding his life safe in his mind. *Add to it*
they said; *it's proof,* speeding up in the hold,

whilst he tries to remember the formula
for acceleration, it's something-ti-something
per second per second. In the box, a snuff

of red soil for the smell of rain already fading,
like the tip of a tongue on a missing tooth.
In the box, the glasses he peeled from his mother's

face, wiped dry on his sleeve, misted with
the breath he couldn't give her. He hears no sound
and it must be everywhere. The woman stares hard

and he can't turn his head. In the box three buttons
he pulled from Nadia's jumper that time after
swimming, brushing her hair. His father's

shoelace given over for the bracelet he made
but never did give, to the girl whose name
he's forgotten, not Maya. Behind him

he knows that half of the aircraft is missing.
People he'll never meet are already many
miles back. He wonders who will be found first.

His certificates in mathematics and languages
the soft firm grip of the visiting professor
per second per second, a stone in a well.

A gecko quick licking its eye, clinging
to the grey green acacia suddenly running
up and up and out of sight.

The spit of soap in the back of his throat,
his mother's arms bent over her knuckles
dragging more water from the twist of the sheets.

His life is so new and so sparkling and happening
now, he wants to offer it to the woman who stares
at him. Give her this gift in mid flight. Almost

laughs at the thought of it, if he could move his lips.

Climate Change

They were arguing in the pub; this old bloke
with the *Telegraph* like a concealed weapon
under his arm, said our estate was named after badgers
so it must have been full of them once,
and Clive's dad said he'd seen one bowling up the Close
and they all laughed because Clive's dad'll say anything
and the old bloke said the trouble was they couldn't adapt,
it's like us with climate change he said we see it coming
but we don't do anything.
So they'd had enough of him then, asked him if he was
lost and he took the hint and left
but me and Clive, we went looking.

We went to the strip of land they call a country park
and we found this place, all scorched blankets and empty tins
and we met a man with a dog who remembered.
He said you'd see them in the road sometimes
dead like, but you'd see them, and once
when he was a kid, when the houses were going up,
he'd heard a mess of men yelling and dogs
having hysterics and when he got there

he saw this circle of men with iron bars, bashing
and bashing at the ground,
dogs bounding around them
snarling at cubs, grabbing at them
jumping at sows and boars,
men and dogs running, bulldogs
and staffs and scrawny Alsatians,
having the time of their lives.

He remembers the blood on their necks,
badgers and dogs, the badgers
running round and round biting at anything
dogs, sticks, each other, making a real fight of it
lads throwing stones, bits of bricks,
and the cubs with dogs on them
hardly recognisable,
like old mats tugged apart,
the badgers slowing down
and the circle widening then shrinking
to a thicket of sticks and bars.
In the end, everyone went home.
He remembers them singing,
hauling the heaviest bits of matting between them.
But that was years ago.

He's not seen a live one since.

After the Tsunami

Since Boxing Day then,
I've been counting the faces
as though to hold on to each one—
in the high tides on Clumber Street
and round by the station
where they're complaining
at the weight of their cases,
the number of things they all own.
And today, I'm in the Meadows,
hemmed in by the snake's curl of river.
I'm walking through subways,
dreaming an avalanche of rubble,
barriers choked with debris,
until it seems strange that pathways are clear,
that shops on Bridgeway sell the same things
they sold last week, to the same people.
I get lost in the masses of houses
all of them lived in, all standing.
I'm counting faces. I didn't know
I could count so high
and the number keeps rising
every one of us alive.

In front of me, a squat black dog
trots through his kingdom,
certain that the Meadows are the whole world,
that the Meadows have always been this way,
and always will be.

The Last Car

No barren landscape after all.
Everything lush as you like.
Hedges stuck their fingers
into walls along the roads,
scattered masonry grew tall.

And the last car knew what it was doing,
or seemed to know, or knew it was the last
and that it had to go.

Afterwards, the grass sprang back.
Reeds were crushed into two black tracks,
sword points angled into water,
mud speckled bright with duckweed
and the hot smell of metal sinking.

And after that the bubbles, heavy as sighs,
then a thin golden stream that caught the light,
and no memory ever of the last slow drive,

leaving the road where the birch had fallen,
bumping gently into the field,
a green ripple in the green.
Everything green for the last car,
leaving the road and bumping gently
through the field to the water's edge.
And in.

The List

I have never been so tired or so cold,
and it's not over yet my friend,
or anything like it.

I am waiting for the day I see your face
in the crowd, or lamp-lit in flickering rain
when stones are thrown through attic bedroom windows,
doors kicked in.

The day the words erupt in the tabloids
and the pavements part.
The day they publish the lists
and invite the paedos out to play.
When we have to choose a side,
declare ourselves.

See you,
you are the magician of the touchline
running onto the pitch with your bucket and magic sponge.
You and the lads, your boys, are ready for this,
ready for the day when teeth are shoved down throats
that want a taste of it. Their own medicine.

Whilst I, I stand dumb on the sidelines,
I cannot move an inch.
One day, my friend, we will have to name our side.
One day my friend, we will all be torn apart.

Part Three: Prison Diary

Day One

I'm exploring the prison, asking
everyone I see for a line from a song.

Upstairs on admin,
well away from the men on the landings,
women rattle with laughter.
They never see the inmates,
if they did, they'd cut a swathe
through the wings hissing poison gas.
I will survive.

Outside the mess, I meet officers
scared to reveal even their eyes.
Their laughter is suspicious, brittle.
I'm living in a cardboard box,
I wish I was a sledgehammer,
I predict a riot.

Out on the wings, they're unembarrassed,
get it straight away.

Jesus loves me.
This time Lord, you gave me a mountain.
Cymru am byth.
The prison boy came home one day
found his true love gone away.

Officer

A young lad this,
cold and bored,
counting them in through the gate,
checking movement slips,
suppressing irritation with older men
who use names instead of numbers,
share jokes.

In his last place
the inmates were less compliant,
gave as good as they got.

He'll knock up a game of pool later,
wear his belt to the pub.
He misses Belmarsh, Leicester,
the action.

First Person

Lunch time lock up's nearly over,
I'm making notes, waiting for Gareth,
whilst over by the desk, the librarians
are shaking out a stack of magazines
looking for porn. Down the road, it's heroin
and razor blades but here it's little girls
and little boys that flutter down
to be recorded, checked on, burnt.

Later, Gareth watches as I read his story—
a man who drinks until his life
goes on without him. You can see
his character will end up in prison, just
maybe not a sex offenders' prison.
I've been struck by something,
revert from reader back to writer.
I really like, she says, *the shift from 'he'
to 'you' the way it ends on 'I'.*

Frowning, Gareth's reading upside down.
An orderly cranks high windows open one by one.
Someone tickers out the pieces of a chess set.
Two men join us in the seating area.
Gareth is exposed—a man undressing
on a windy beach. He's sending signals,
begging his reader to stop talking,

but she's gripped by this idea. *It reads*
she says, *like a confession, almost
unconscious.* Prison protocol, especially
this prison's protocol,
does not let him sit closer or say
shut up, shut the fuck up, people are listening.
But he's safe, she's shut up already,
already she's at work and writing in her head.

Very soon, she'll realise that Gareth's change
in person wasn't meant and that he thinks
she's made a fool of him.
Just before it dawns on her,
she thinks she's gained an insight
into inmates' writing
and at the very moment Gareth decides
never to risk this kind of thing again,
she's thinking of all the other times
a person might not want
to start their story using 'I'.

The Folk Singer

He pulls off his hat,
resettles it, pleads with the air,
knows better than to miss his tablets
or forget his bible.

He still thinks about
the thing he did, a long time ago.
The horrors of his life before that.

And after all these years,
like a long game of patience,
he lays out his excuses.

At six years old
waking in a cold place to blinding light,
leather straps,
adults without mouths bending together.
The stink of ether.

The terrible cold shoulder of his mother,
how she handed him to the priests.
The sea bucking under the boat into exile.
Those years alone in London
doing the things the priests taught him
after all.

He lays them down
like a game of patience
that won't come out.

He pulls off his hat,
resettles it, pleads with the air.
Finally, slowly,
he holds up his hands.

Toe By Toe

Is the reading
scheme, inmates
teaching
in mates
where part
of a word
rep eats
part
of a
word
nev
er reach ing
a full sent
ence
and

Toe by Toe's
the name
I've given him
this man of mothballs and patience
who coats my tongue with cod liver oil
and only wants, he says,
a chance to teach,
then tells me it's a relief
to have intelligent conversation.

It's not only that he lies,
or that he tries, and does, impress:
all that power in his past,
it's his assumption that I haven't guessed
what he wants from me.

Aha, he says in his dreams,
aha aha aha
is iss is iss.
He only wants the chance to teach.

And he reads me well,
linseed putty under his fat thumb,
he sniffs his fingertips and smiles.
But I can read minds too.

I know he thinks I'm his way in,
I know he thinks
I'll recommend him for the scheme,
I know he thinks himself half starved.

I know he dreams young men
who can't yet read.

What He Says Is

See, all he's saying is, maybe what you need here is training in poverty and solitude. How to be happy on sod all with no-one. There are men in here who've given up, turned their faces to the wall. You, with your programmes and psychology, you call them defeatist, you treat them as though they're dead already. But *he* says what those men have is serenity. He reckons he turned a corner last week when he stopped writing those fantasies and started making things out of matches. He says most men in here pretend it's not there or else think they're the ones to climb over it. They'll give in to hope again and again. But what about those other men, the ones with sloping shoulders who don't look up, who shovel down their food and never ask for seconds. They're the ones we should be proud of, that's what he says. They're the ones with real courage, the ones who see what lies ahead, he says, and face the wall.

Smoking Ban

Outside the dog compound,
Jackie hands me a piece of paper
clean folded to a knife edge —
a simple prayer, for anyone to read.
Is it multi-faith enough she asks,
it's for their rehabilitation.
Maybe one of them can read it,
stop them topping themselves.

She's cross-eyed with inhaling,
streaming smoke.
Mind you, she says,
it doesn't bother me if they do,
but you didn't hear that.

She types reports,
minute-by-minute thoughts
of men whose offences
she also types, minute-by-minute.
And then their progress
through psychology, sees
how vocabularies shift.

Once, she tried to tell her husband.
Don't tell me he said,
there's no point,
it won't get it out of your head.
So she smokes.

She'll scrape back her chair,
batter down the stairs,
grate her keys through all those doors
to lock herself outside,
stamping on thoughts,

grinding out words she's typed
and can't repeat.

They've told her it's the law now,
offered her nicotine patches
given her an inhaler but you can't
storm off out with them.

So she'll smoke against the ban,
against the dog wire,
and they can sack her she says,
they can sack her.

Substantially Enclosed

I'm chain smoking outside The Dragon,
substantially enclosed on two sides,
a white walled corner facing the fire escape,
receding rooflines, four chimneys neatly stacked.
Behind them, a sky, belatedly blue,
and beside me, a bunch of flowers so huge
people eye me with suspicion,
think I'm trying to sell them. But I've left my job,
it's the end of something, a release date.

In the prison, men set out chairs in a semi circle
and read to each other. Big men, sweating with nerves,
wires exposed. And then the clapping, which was real
and a kind of triumph, but it all feels like the end game.

I'm thinking of the spider guarding Tate Modern
on pincer legs, of how I looked up once,
between them, to the tendons on Millennium Bridge.
If she hatched the eggs she carries, they'd cling
together for a while, staples ripped from magazines,
then they'd trust to the wind, stick to St. Paul's,
The Eye, scutter down drains on Fleet Street.

I walked the North Bank, drawn to the muscle of water,
felt its desire to rise so strong, I had to look away,
study instead, the idle lapping at Blackfriars Bridge.
And that night, back outside the Tate,
the spider blackly fronts projections of future tides,
blue-lit lines on buildings around London,
the drownings to come.

I didn't think I'd go back to the prison,
didn't think of anything much,
the rising water, the semi circle of chairs,
these outlandish flowers.

Time becomes crooked, two cities at once.
I have no idea what order things come in,

and whatever people say,
or pay to have displayed on hoardings,
it's not writing that sets you free,
it's the end of the sentence.

Part Four: Demolition

How To Begin a Person

Take a night where the canvas rips,
where something stumbles outside in the dark
and plastic chairs somersault in sheeting rain
snagged by windbreak beech at the field's edge.

A night in which, in any case,
you would not have slept
when you are pushing wet feet into boots
to check guy ropes, hammer in pegs,
soaked in seconds and back inside
for a shuddering cup of red wine.

So it's a seduction of sorts,
an unguarding under a rocking light,
odd glimpses of knees and belly,
a concertinaing of sleeping bags.

In the morning, we rest on the beach,
the storm's memory a fidget in the waves.
You are laid out on the rocks
heavy with hangover.
I am lying on the sea's soft edge,
dreaming of Zeus in a shower of light
turning into restless salt water
And in that moment, the beginnings of the child
who will always be
the calm beyond the storm.

Boy

When did that happen then? So quick.
Do you remember, that soft insistent
nudging of the mattress to wake us up?
Eyes round, pyjamas unbalanced.

And then his drawings,
countless Roman soldiers
falling stiff bodied off his cliffs.
Those grinning pirates.

And later, for hours and hours
the gentle clicking of Lego.
Padded up for roller hockey,
skating backwards, that distant curve.

And homework and homework,
companionable cups of tea, and then
just now, on his way to bed, looking down,
he sees me drawing again

and he says,
you'll never sell one.
I'm trying, if you remember,
to draw sounds. To wake me up.

Wisteria banging against the window
the rattle of the cat on the ironing board
the restless huff of the dog
and the sound of a boy, growing.

Thirteen and a Half

Everywhere she goes now,
boys bay at her with broken voices,
they follow her on bikes, feet scuffing pavements,
veering round the shocked remains of council trees,
or slowly, in cars, windows sliding down.

Grown men watch as she passes,
with eyes like damp hands
heavy on her back.
And what did she do for this
but grow a little older?

She walks stiff-legged,
arms across her chest,
hair swinging, to shield her eyes.
It tires her out, this walk
that used to ease her in from school to home.
They make her wade upstream.

Is she supposed to pick just one,
to hold the others off?
Sometimes she'd like to turn with the current
and close her eyes, let her hair flow behind her,
whilst ahead and all unseen—
white water boiling at the rapids,
black rocks jagged.

Summer of Rain

He's going home on the Fifteen,
trying to think in A level German, but the words
get stuck on the back of his throat.

There are times, when the sun
shines just right on the waste ground,
that his fingers still itch
for the rattle of matches, the scrape of a lighter,
when he thinks through his skin
of great black plumes of smoke
from abandoned tyres.

But this is the summer of rain,
and in any case, that was years ago.
He thinks he may get off at a different stop,
walk through warm rain to her house,
arrive at the leaf litter of her front door
his hair dripping in her smile.

But she's heading towards him,
on the Fifteen going the other way.
She said to her mum she'd be back for five
but she thinks instead she'll get off at his stop,
cram her failed umbrella into a bin
with its spokes like bat bones sticking through skin
and walk through the rain to his house,
arrive with her jeans soaked up to her knees
like sails flapping after a heavy sea.

The sky towers grey over the High School playing fields,
over the trees beyond Ridgeway;
if their need to see each other is equally strong,
they won't.

Like Dyslexia

His brother's back at Uni, head down over his fourth pint.
He'll be fretting over genetics—got an IQ as high as the
tower of Babel
and reading makes him sick.

Younger sister's still upstairs, hammering sense
into her drums, she thinks, if she stays there long enough,
they'll learn the blood beat of her walls,
a pulse that she can change at will.

The eldest left home years ago, got out as early as she could,
and tries, from time to time, to get back in—like the SAS,
smashing windows, lobbing in stun grenades,
tear gas canisters hissing round the living room

whilst parental eyes are fixed on screens,
pedantic fingers on the keyboard—control, alt, delete,
or blatant, sleeping through the evening news.
For years and years they did their best, and now,
no longer knowing how that goes,
they take their ease.

And as for him, he's riding low,
slumped in the back of his mate's geared up Astra,
cruising the circuits of the city streets,
girls blurred at the railings, headphones jammed in place,
thinking every day's the day he won't go home.
He's hearing what he wants to hear,
seeing with his eyes closed.
He knows that everything is
absolutely up to him.

Tomb Raider

It's going to be another evening in.
Early January, untangling the wires,
scurfing the dust from old games.
What is it we're trying to remember?

He's killing wolves again, firing her pistols
falling through floors, picking up secrets.
The coals have shivered grey, heated
up the room to swell the air between us.

We keep doors and windows closed,
could do with a howl of wind
a flurry of snow to pucker the hearth.

I am reading the poems of Ezra Pound.
A scratchy bitchiness prevails.

Cleave

after all, is not a Janus word,
looking two ways,
it's dual meanings kiss with tongues
making more than any single word
could hold.

And so the stunned and faithful child
staggers back towards the sofa and the hand
that hacked his babyhood in two.

And so, in London, a Somali woman buckles, breathless,
glimpsing patterns on a cloth her memory won't sanction
whilst the longing for them turns her legs to lead.

And so, at the end of the marriage,
clinging to the axe that found the line of weakness,
this fool of a woman
this idiot man.

Demolition

And any time I pause today,
stomping through wet playing fields
up to Ally Pally,
retracing steps in Highgate Woods,

I picture fences caving in, bulldozers
lumbering towards my trees back home.
Behind this sessile oak, visions of my Judas tree,
yanked out by its roots,

Soon enough the wrecking fist
will slam against the wall
where fifteen years ago I painted Viking ships,

and in my garden now, hellebore,
snakes head fritillaries, crocuses,
cohorts of daffodils
planted one by one by one.

Rain comes as I look for Highgate Cemetery
past construction sites
where men shelter amongst breezeblocks.
I see my chimney topple, slates attached,
but maybe they'll dismantle brick by brick by brick.

The cemetery's an ivy carpet wood
graves crammed like mushrooms,
I think if I could twist and lift them up,
they'd all grow back
as I must try to do,
jetlagged with indecision.

In Waterlow Park, I ask directions again,
and again, I get them, concise, trustworthy,
as though Londoners always know
precisely where they are.

I approach Hornsey over Archway, through Crouch End.
Behind me, getting closer, the rumble of demolition,
thirty years of marriage crumbling.

I could take up each bulb, dig out the fireplace,
dismantle piece by piece.
I could pack a single bag and go.
I could be decisive as a Londoner.

But I'm writing this in Hornsey
and this pub is called the Wishing Well.

Wrong Word

You don't have the word you need right now,
between oblivion, absent without leave,
but 'suicide' you have receptors for,
a word your body answers readily.
And once you let it in, it flirts and grins,
will nudge you to another midnight wine,
and though you're pretty sure the word is wrong,
you don't believe the right one's been defined.
You raise a brimming toast to certainty,
swilling down the dregs of restless guilt
and one night, almost absentmindedly,
you take the leap, the razor blade, the pill.
You needed one more word, when all are said,
to want to die, but not to end up dead.

Part Five: The Maze

Every Thursday

The machine for making holes
vibrates the tarmac as the point goes in.
He's watching from the road for cracks
but none appear, the ground absorbs the fury
and he knows that his face too, is calm.

Cranes are everywhere erasing memory,
disseminating change.
Nottingham's a flick book and he hasn't got a clue.
Even names he knows confuse him,
bruises that he hasn't touched in years.
Pretty Windows, William IV.

Walking up from town, he leaves it to his feet
to find pavements he remembers.
He passes high Victorian houses where,
—he can't quite put his finger on it—
respect or anger may be due;
tries a paper shop, he thinks at random,
and the man there knows his name,
We don't sell your Capstan Full Strength, Jack,
we never will.
He wonders vaguely if Mohammedans
read minds but otherwise is unsurprised,
walks down narrow roads he's never seen before
until his feet find cobbles
as his fingers find his keys.

Baden Powell Road
exactly where he left it.

The Maze

Turn left. He is bringing you seven red roses.
When you take them from him you
will know what he is trying to say.
Left again.
He will hand you seven round red roses
and he will say—
Right. He will take the bull by the horns and he will say—
But of course, you might *not* know.

Left. It is close to evening. The yew hedges darken their angles.
Long ago he did cross almost seven seas.
Right and then Left.
He was thirteen when he came. He remembers
that sweets were less sticky, that English sheep
had heavier fleeces and lessons were a little easier.
He became a foreigner much later.

He is bringing you five round red roses.
A hand span of roses.
Because he reached out his hand and you took it. A friend
ship. Again, Left. What if it is nothing more than a friendship?
The roses have no scent. Right and then Left. And a dead end.
It is close to evening, his good raincoat absorbs a little of the green.
Right.
What if, after all these years, maybe in these exact
circumstances, this raincoat could be just slightly.
Left. UnEnglish?

And he has done well.
There is no harm in doing well.
Left. He brings you twelve perfect roses.
He has a desire to blunder his face into the scentless roses.
It is close to evening. He is blundering towards you,
a vegetarian in a china shop. Left.

You are in the centre of the maze,
and he is a red-cheeked schoolboy
offering you these preposterous flowers.
Three red roses.
He is cautious, uncertain, supremely confident. Left again.
And you love him, despise him, mock him, revere him,
do not need him. It is evening. He will not find you at night.

He is bringing you seven red roses.

On Football and Killing Chickens
21st June 2002

So, I'm at the bus stop stunned and only half awake.
All I know is, it's 2:1 to Brazil and not over yet.
It was 1:1 at the cob shop, shutters up, no customers,
quiet as though we're muffled by a foot of snow.
At the post office, they watched it on the black and white,
nervous as another break in.

It was Owen who woke me up—that roar from the factory,
I thought it was on fire again—then I remembered.

And now I'm on the bus. A woman
tells me about killing sick chickens in Jamaica,
performing post mortems on hens.

She said they got so thin the wind blew them over.
She found kinks like bent fingers in the intestines,
coconut straw in the gizzards.
Fascinated her to the knifepoint.

Her husband used to work at Boots,
big man, strong man, heavy manual,
had to be dragged off every shift,
and then he got thin,
and she knew before he did, before the doctors did—
because of things the chickens taught her.

If he'd lived, they might have—
she gets off at the Chinese wholesalers

and we're in town and I know it's over.
Don't have to ask. Can't ask.
Streets full of people and I'm walking
into a wall of sadness.

A man leans against the railings on Parliament Street
opposite a flag in a café window,
can't look at it, has to stand opposite.
He's too weak to stand.

Somebody comes over to him, could be anybody,
stands really close, doesn't put his arm round
but the arm's there.

And I'm here alone, with this misery
lapping over my ankles sucking me in,
I'm losing my grip and I have to remember,
this has nothing to do with me.
If there was a wind, it would blow me over.

Winter Solstice

On the outer edge of Mablethorpe,
over bungalows on Jacklin Close
the wind farm stands sentinel.

Behind garage doors
mobility scooters tick to silence,
the clatter of plates washed and dried,
is put away as tellies dim
as bathroom doors sigh shut
on the final flush, as beds creak
and glass conservatories stare back
at the darkest night of the year.

Golf Road, to the beach car park,
snow dusted, fox scavenged,
the café barricaded against sand and salt,
where the wind gets up, shakes its mane,
rolls restless over marram tufted dunes,
bounds across Lincoln fields
towards midwinter midnight,

and wakes the turbines up.
The wind growls a greeting,
leaps to embrace as towers wrench and sway,
and rotors turn, begin the solstice dance
inherited from standing stones,
from the Orkneys down to Wiltshire.

Over by the sewage works,
cats flatten against gateposts,
barn owls perch and close their eyes
as Time pulls back for the giants
and the lion wind

and bungalows sleep sound
'til time lets go,
and the wind falls back exhausted.

Milk floats whine
as curtains rattle back
on newly trampled hedges,
on new lines scored in heavy clay.

On the wind farm,
that much closer.

The Naming of Plants

The secateurs from Spear and Jackson,
because the sun shone, danced the dust,
warmed my back. The pruning of the roses,
was I early? Or just too late?

Cutting back slantwise to an outward facing bud,
the white that overthrew the peach
to balance and explain.
Because my father, in *his* garden . . .
And now they hang, the buds
grey coated, spreading grey, and will not open.

Because the rain came, the wind and the rain,
for days and days on wounds I had not treated,
on bushes still in shock. The wind threshing
and the rain and the garden hanging.

Because my father in *his* garden . . .
Old man hates nasturtiums,
no reason, chrysanthemums no better,
but cyclamen, out in the snow, peering close,
he drinks a toast to the first ones out.

I think I thought to take the reins, the broad
thumb to pinch the leaves and rub,
plant when the soil is warm to the bum,
acanthus in the sun,
thymus minimus between the slabs.

Because my father in *his* garden —
the names of the plants in his garden . . .
The buds hang grey and will not open
and the garden is heavy and the rain came.
I have cut away the very branch the
honeysuckle would have clung

to. And the rose roots rot. Because
for my own garden, I thought I would know.
And now I am out in this glistening midnight
I am pushing wet roots into a black plastic bag.

The grey buds that would not open.
I stuff the mess into a bin.
Because my father is beginning to forget
the names of the plants in his garden.

Separation

This child's an odd one though, he lives
in a trick of the light, so I've never met his
Siamese twin, although I think he's got one.

See him flicker on the swing, dipping
his toes in the apple light. He's here, and there.
Same head, same body, same legs, different Dad.

I'm picking raspberries snagged in the sun.
He tells me, whilst he's busy stamping down
a cloud of meadow grass to stringy green,

that Daddy Jason's over twelve feet tall
and owns an army knife as big as Wales.
And Daddy Steve? He scowls and scuffs dry earth.

I glance upwards, frowning in the sun,
attempt in hedgerow silences to calculate
the drifting hours and watch him run

all urgent, self-important through the beans.
Elbows out, hands working loose, he's running
crooked, like an imitation fast kid.

I've never met his Siamese twin although
he's got one. I should think he lives alone
in the dust behind the allotments where

Daddy Jason hides at night, crouching, arms
outstretched, listening, listening, for Daddy Steve.

What if the Ransom's Set Too High?

What if the ransom's set too high?
If they made you pawn your future
and your past, if you lost the ticket
and have no way, in any case,
of redeeming it.

What if the door they hid from you
slams shut, no handle,
and you sold your fingernails.

They take you into one more empty room,
tell you one more time,
not to fool yourself with hope.

What if, in odd unguarded moments,
you too make plans to bury him,
reject them angrily at first,
then out of habit, clinging on.

They stripped you bare,
made you burn the furniture,
the chairs you no longer
remember him making.

One by one, you tear pages
from albums to feed the fire
that does not make you warm.

And what if then, they give him back,
bundled from the car you thought
was just another siren in the night.

He's blank-eyed, bloodied,
needing you.
What then?

Castaway

You have to remember this man:
worked the North Sea,
months on, months off,
arms like drift wood, salt eyed,
sat up rigid as the oxygen tank,
lungs bleached to burning.

The way you thought he'd fade,
washed up like that in hospital pyjamas,
the way, after only a couple of nights,
he pulled himself up to walk,
to take his neighbour's teeth
and clean them, so careful,
you pictured him lifting hooks
from the mouths of minnows.

And the next night,
not to trouble the nurses,
he fetched a blanket
for the old man opposite
before carting himself off
down the corridor to smoke outside.
And the old man's old wife,
who stood with him,
because she used to smoke herself,
the way he reassured her
told her he'd be there a week or so,
and get the blanket, call the nurses
so she was safe to go home for the night.

And nobody stopped him smoking,
even after the ban, and you have to hope
he's at sea now,
you have to wish him that.

Lost and Found

Last August I fell down the stairs
and moved into a new country.

I lost the tick of the gas fire,
my hand reaching for the right book

for a land of visitors on plastic chairs,
the blue gown tied at the back.

I fell down stairs, I lost my voice,
my body and I became strangers.

I find bright lights, the clang of bins,
and with each new ward, a change in ceiling fan.

I lost the taste of sugar snap peas
picked as water boils, the rub of mint.

I have found the tracheotomy tube,
the rasp of salt at the back of my throat.

The kind of people I would once avoid,
find nurses for me in the middle of the night.

I have lost my voice. I find my wife
reads well out loud, I find she knows

when to ask the difficult questions
when to let things be. I find her kisses

mean more to me each day. Each day
she tells me how proud I make her.

And it's wonderful to have lived this long
to have found this out about each other.

The Wind

I have hollowed out a place for myself
and still it tries to get in between the sand dunes
and the bookcase—the wind that circles the room,
throwing gravel rain at my windows,

skittering slates on the rain-black roof,
and I will not remember, on days like these,
on nights like these, the ringing of the mobile phones.

Letters in the hall are buried under piles of sand,
I half expect the flapping of fish
sliding down towards the kitchen door.

Outside the wind blows,
and beyond the wood,
grasses ripple too fast
for cloud shadow.

The wind has brought the sand
to slide between my fingers.
I will let it scratch my eyes
stop up my mouth.
I have dug myself a hollow
and still it tries to get in.

You Tell Me That the Dead Are Dead

You tell me that the dead are dead, and I believe you,
bones and ashes, but you named your son for him
as he named his, you send your tremors down the wires,
a lullaby to ease them through their sleep, and I believe

no memory's too faint to wake the dead. I believe
in strangers touching strangers in the jolting of the tram,
an eyebrow raised in such a way, an accent
unremembered from a parent's youth, and everything

remains within the landscape. The power of name
whispers through limestone, threads smoke from tree to tree
and what's buried in the roots rises with the sap
to be exhaled, consumed by sun, absorbed by rain.

Even in the names of trees the past returns:
Cedar of Lebanon, English Oak, Mountain Ash.

Lightning Source UK Ltd.
Milton Keynes UK
01 March 2011

168463UK00001B/28/P